Meditations for
the Expectant Mother

Herald Press
Meditation Books

By Helen Good Brenneman
Meditations for the Expectant Mother
Meditations for the New Mother

By John M. Drescher
Meditations for the Newly Married

By John Delbert Erb
God's Word for All Nations

By Sara Wenger Shenk and N. Gerald Shenk
Meditations for New Parents

By Vernell Klassen Miller
Meditations for Adoptive Parents

By Susanne Coalson Donoghue
Meditations for Single Moms

By Various Authors
Visitation Pamphlet Series

Meditations for the Expectant Mother

Revised Edition

HELEN GOOD BRENNEMAN

Drawings by
ESTHER ROSE GRABER

A book of inspiration for the mother-to-be

HERALD PRESS
Scottdale, Pennsylvania
Waterloo, Ontario

MEDITATIONS FOR THE EXPECTANT MOTHER
Copyright © 1968, 1985, by Herald Press, Scottdale, PA 15683
    Published simultaneously in Canada by Herald Press,
    Waterloo, Ont. N2L 6H7. All rights reserved
Library of Congress Catalog Card Number: 68-12025
International Standard Book Numbers:
    0-8361-1567-8 (softcover)
    0-8361-1639-9 (hardcover)
Printed in the United States of America

Thirty-second printing, 1998
225,500 copies in print

To Loretta

Contents

Author's Preface

It seemed like a step backward to write this book for expectant mothers fifteen years after the publication of the first edition of *Meditations for the New Mother*.

However, since God has blessed the book for new mothers in a way which none of us anticipated, it was suggested that a companion volume for the mother while waiting for the birth of the baby might also be well received. For new motherhood's joys and problems begin, not with the birth of the child, but with conception, when the miracle of birth begins within the mother's body. Then great expectations dawn upon her soul.

For every season of life, for every high and low experience, there comes a word from the Lord, a message of hope and comfort. *Meditations for the Expectant Mother* is a collection of inspiration for that special nine-month chapter of pregnancy. Although it is written for the expectant mother, we hope that the "expectant" father will benefit also at least indirectly, from its message.

When should these meditations be read? I would suggest that the expectant mother read through the volume the first thirty days after she receives it, returning to specific meditations when she feels a particular need.

To expectant mothers, as well as to nurses, doctors, and other friends who read the manuscript and offered suggestions and encouragement, I express my sincere appreciation. And for you, Expectant Mother, I offer a prayer that these meditations will, as our Quaker friend would say it, "speak to your condition."

Helen Good Brenneman
Goshen, Indiana

Miracle in the Making

"Fearfully and wonderfully made."
Psalm 139:14

FOR AN UNBORN CHILD

I pray God
In the hour of my pain
For this our child
Born of our bone,
Fashioned of our flesh,
Yet—mystery of God—
An immortal soul . . . .

That he might know
Sweetness and warming at his mother's breast;
That he might grow
Wise, kind, benevolent beneath his father's hand;
That he might live
Before God's face
To goodly age spent following righteous ways.

What more to ask of God
For this our child
Born of our bone,
Fashioned of our flesh,
Yet—mystery of God—
An immortal soul. [1]

Miriam Sieber Lind

1. The Wonder of It All!

She knew that other women had given birth to babies. She had been in her teens when the last baby brother came.

But somehow this was different. Marie could never get over the wonder of it—that a tiny, living individual was being formed within her own body, that she was a partner with God in creation of a living soul! This new person would be part of herself and all her ancestors and part of her husband and all of his.

She sat down with the article which she had clipped from a recent magazine. It described just what was going on within her. Although she had never been particularly interested in biology, she had devoured charts on pregnancy. A miracle it was—life evolving without any help from her, a miracle of God.

It had surprised her, when she first learned that she was pregnant, that already her baby, at four weeks, was beginning to form internal organs—heart, liver, digestive system, brain, and lungs. The heart was already beating, although too faint to be heard. All this in a baby no bigger than a quarter of an inch in length! She had marked the measurement on her ruler. At six weeks, when she had moved the mark to half an inch, it thrilled her to know that her baby now had arms and legs. By week seven the ears and eyelids were forming, the internal organs moving into place, and the embryo floating in a bag of waters.

Now, as she entered the fourth month, she marked two and one half inches on her ruler and tried to imagine the fetus, with fingers and toes, tiny nails beginning to show, hair starting to grow on a tiny head, and teeth beginning to form within the gums. How she wished she knew whether the baby was a boy or girl!

Oh, the wonder of it all! Taking her Bible from the shelf, Marie read aloud.

For you created my inmost being;
   you knit me together in my mother's
     womb.
I praise you because I am fearfully
   and wonderfully made;
   your works are wonderful,
   I know that full well.
My frame was not hidden from you
   when I was made in the secret place.

When I was woven together in the
   depths of the earth,
   your eyes saw my unformed body.
All the days ordained for me
   were written in your book
   before one of them came to be.
How precious to me are your
   thoughts, O God!

Psalm 139:13-17a

Somehow, it gave her a feeling of security to know that God, forming a baby within her, also knew the child's future and had a plan for this life. Bowing her head, she thanked her Maker and prayed his blessing upon her unborn child.

"I praise you. . . . Your works are wonderful. . . . How precious to me are your thoughts, O God!" Loving Father, help my child to know you and the joy of living in your will. Amen.

THE BABY

Where did you come from, baby dear?
Out of the everywhere into the here.

Where did you get your eyes so blue?
Out of the sky as I came through.

What makes the light in them sparkle and spin?
Some of the starry spikes left in.

Where did you get that little tear?
I found it waiting when I got here.

What makes your forehead so smooth and high?
A soft hand stroked it as I went by.

What makes your cheek like a warm white rose?
Something better than anyone knows.

Whence that three-cornered smile of bliss?
Three angels gave me at once a kiss.

Where did you get that pearly ear?
God spoke, and it came out to hear.

Where did you get those arms and hands?
Love made itself into hooks and bands.

Feet, whence did you come, you darling things?
From the same box as the cherubs' wings.

How did they all just come to be you?
God thought about me, and so I grew.

But how did you come to us, you dear?
God thought of you, and so I am here.

George MacDonald

14

2. A Living Soul

A preschooler on a popular TV program was asked what he thought heaven was like. "There are a lot of babies there," he responded, "waiting to be born."

We might question this little boy's theology, but we know that every baby is an immortal soul, a "VIP," a person created in the image of God. Even before birth the human fetus is precious, for a potential human being is evolving, a Self, a Someone who will live on into eternity. Jesus Christ recognized the child as an important person. He paid attention to children, blessed them, used them as object lessons for adults, and taught that each child has an angel in heaven, always beholding the face of the Father.

What does it mean when the Bible tells us that we are created in the image of God? Surely this image is blurred in most of us! But a human baby differs from an animal baby. A human is given the freedom to make choices, a mind capable of thinking things through, a personality which will live on even after death, and a conscience which can be trained to distinguish between good and evil. Through Jesus Christ this human personality can gradually grow more like the Father, more in the image of the one who is love.

The importance of bringing into the world such a creature of choice is staggering. Perhaps there ought to be an inauguration ceremony, with pomp and circumstance, for every new parent. After a solemn speech on the challenge of parenthood, the father and mother might respond in the following manner (reworded from the response of an incoming college president): "It is a high privilege to be here and to accept the emblem of my office and with the responsibilities.... I promise to bring my energies, imagination, and such talents as I possess to this office.... I express to you my resolve to serve this family faithfully, and seek God's guidance to that end."

The Bible says, "And the Lord God formed man from the dust of the ground and breathed into his nostrils the breath of life, and man became a living being" (Genesis 2:7). My theologian friend tells me that in Hebrew a living *soul* means a living *creature*. This creature is a unified personality, comprised of body, soul, and spirit. Alta Erb and Winifred Paul, in their *Christian Parents Baby Book*,[2] quote the famous words of Patri, "Do a good job the first three years and you take out a good insurance for the years ahead." But they add this word of wisdom, "Human infancy and childhood are extended over many years. God has given time to make [an adult]."

If the coming baby would arrive unannounced in a basket on our doorstep, the infant would be no more a mystery than the one being prepared within the mother's body. The training of that "living creature" is our solemn task as parents.

"Grant, O Father of all, that Thy holy angels, as they do always behold Thy face in heaven, may evermore protect Thy little ones on earth from every danger, both of body and soul; through Jesus Christ our Lord. Amen" (S. Gladstone, 1844).[3]

POWER IN WEAKNESS

"My power is made perfect in weakness"

2 Corinthians 12:9

O Lord, save this woman thy servant;
    Who putteth her trust in thee.
Be thou to her a strong tower;
    From the face of her enemy.
Lord, hear our prayer,
    And let our cry come unto thee.
        Amen[4]

3. A Spiritual Layette

And she "being great with child." How often, since childhood, Muriel had read those lines in her Bible (Luke 2:5, KJV). But today the words became real to her personally.

Driving downtown for a few bargains, Muriel had attempted to park in a slanting, parallel parking space. It turned out that the space was large enough for her car, but not for her! First, she tried getting out on the driver's side, only to discover that there was not enough room between cars for her clumsy frame. Sliding across the seat, Muriel tried the other side, again to discover that she couldn't get out. After checking to be sure no one she knew had seen her predicament, Muriel looked for another parking place, chuckling to herself as she drove down the street.

Only that week Muriel's doctor had announced that the baby could come anytime now, and asked whether she was ready. She had answered in the affirmative, knowing that, with the help of a baby shower, her drawers were filled with soft, pastel garments—a beautiful layette.

Now, driving home, Muriel wondered if she were really ready—ready in other ways for this child. She had read all the books and thought she knew what to expect on D-Day (Delivery Day, for her). Having had younger brothers and sisters, she even felt a bit confident in her ability to care for the little one when she would get him home. But often during her pregnancy Muriel had wondered about her baby's spiritual layette. How quickly she could turn her thoughts in upon herself, becoming absorbed in her own aches and pains or her own comforts! With the coming of the baby, she would need resources of strength—more patience, unselfishness, guidance, and humble dependence upon God.

Muriel had tried to live with equanimity, had prayed for spiritual maturity. In a few days or weeks, the little one would be facing a new world, a world of her own and Harold's making. What kind of spiritual layette had she prepared?

That night Muriel confided in Harold her feelings of inadequacy for the job ahead. "I know we're ready for the baby in the little things," she said, "but how about in the ways that really count? It seems to me that I have so much to learn before I'm fit to be a mother."

Harold admitted that he felt the same about fatherhood. "But," he said thoughtfully, "I remember the prayer of Solomon, and how he felt before he undertook the job of being king." Together Harold and Muriel read the words from 1 Kings 3:7, 9:

"Now, O Lord my God, you have made your servant king in place of my father David. But I am only a little child and do not know how to carry out my duties.... So give your servant a discerning heart."

"I suppose, Muriel," Harold said, "that if we were perfect parents, we would be the first. We'll make plenty of mistakes, but we can pray for an understanding mind."

O Lord our God, wise we aren't; mature—not as much as we should be; good—not in ourselves. Give your servants therefore an understanding mind. Amen.

A CHRISTIAN HOME

"Enjoy life with the wife whom you love . . . ."
"Live . . . in harmony with one another . . . with one voice glorify . . . God."

O God, make the door of this house wide enough to receive all who need human love and fellowship; narrow enough to shut out all envy, pride, and strife.

Make its threshold smooth enough to be no stumbling block to children, nor to straying feet, but rugged and strong enough to turn back the tempter's power. God make the door of this house the gateway to Thine eternal kingdom.[5]

4. The Making of Parents

Some years ago a father-to-be wrote an article on "How to Live with a Pregnant Wife." I don't remember his advice in detail, but I do remember his going out into the night to satisfy his wife's craving for hamburger. This young husband learned that babies complicate married life even before they are born!

The authors of *Your New Baby and You*,[6] point out that during pregnancy the wife has special worries: about her figure, how she will behave in labor, the baby's and her own welfare, her ability to be a good mother. But the husband, too, has worries. He sometimes worries for fear he might not get his wife to the hospital in time, whether the doctor is competent; how their lives will be changed, whether he will be a good father, and will the baby come first with his wife? Couples worry together about money, household space, marital relations, being tied down, and disruption of their lives.

One of the problems of young parenthood is that we are still making adjustments to one another while at the same time adjusting to a new member of the family. For the wife this may be doubly difficult, especially since she may not always be feeling her best. Breakfast smells may drive her out of the house, or she may be quickly tired and irritable, or she may find herself strangely emotional over little things.

"I'll be laughing one minute with my husband and child," one wife wrote to a friend, "and the next thing I know I am crying."

If, however, the couple has gone into marriage with the realistic idea of "for better or for worse," neither husband nor wife will expect life to be always sunshine and apple pie. They will accept each other's frailties and limitations and work at their marriage in a creative way.

It has been said that "the best thing a father can do for his children is to make their mother happy." This can also be said to wives—making the father secure in their love is most important in bringing up a happy family. Although children consume a great deal of time and energy, a couple must be careful not to neglect one another. For the future of children is dependent upon the continuation and growth of the love which begot them.

Early marriage is the time to establish patterns of life: talking things over, dreaming together, showing affection, thinking about goals and family ideals, and above all praying together.

While it takes God only nine months to make a baby, it seems, it takes a lifetime to make a parent!

Definition of a baby: That which makes the home happier,
love stronger, patience greater,
hands busier, nights longer, days
shorter, purses lighter, clothes
shabbier, the past forgotten,
the future brighter.
Marion Lawrence

19

HANNAH, SEWING

I like to think of Hannah at her window,
Stitching the little coat she was to take
To the small child Samuel housed within the temple,
And the yearly pilgrimage she was to make
Drawing near, until her preparations
Were all but ready, save this one small thing:
The little coat she made for her beloved,
To bless and cheer him with its comforting.

Seam by tiny seam she did her stitching,
But often through her tears her eyes were dim,
For though she bravely kept her sacred promise
To give him up, she could but long for him.
Motherlike she yearned to hold her baby,
Close to her heart—to tuck him into bed—
She reached her arms across the miles to fold him,
Then she knew the coat must warm her child, instead.[7]
Grace Noll Crowell

5. She Bargained with God

Read 1 Samuel, chapters 1 and 2:1-26.

Oh, Hannah, I know a little of how you felt. I too waited awhile to become pregnant, long enough to experience empathy with those who wait and wait, never to be rewarded for their patience. And the frustration, the disappointment, the bitterness of spirit, only another woman knows.

Elkanah was a good husband to you, but even he did not understand. The priest in the temple was sympathetic, but his spirit did not walk the valley of despair with you. I have heard men discuss your motives in wanting a child, and I had to laugh. What did they know of your yearning, the intense longing of your heart? For you suffered as only a would-be mother fully understands.

I don't know which of you, dear Hannah, was the more miserable, you or your rival, Peninnah. For while she bore Elkanah's children, you had his love. In your bitterness you probably forgot, Hannah, that her lot was hardest. Although she enjoyed the love of her children, she could never find fulfillment being second in the life of Elkanah. No wonder she taunted you with her insinuations and meannesses!

We who have waited for motherhood know how you felt. Every time you saw a mother toting a diaper bag, or a friend surrounded by small children, you asked yourself, "What does she have that I don't have? Why is God so good to her? Am I a terrible sinner, or inadequate as a woman, that God has not blessed me with a child?" And every time "that time of month" rolled around, you knew fresh depression and disappointment, so that you were hard to live with, even for patient Elkanah.

In our modern world we can't understand what it would be like to share a husband, but we can imagine, Hannah, that it was particularly difficult for you when *she* announced that she was expecting again. It must have been the last straw!

But Hannah, you prayed. In your agony you cried to the Lord. Were you bargaining with him, as someone has suggested? Well, maybe you were, but God did not reprimand you for it. He took you up on your promise, gave you a child, and blessed a nation through the life of that boy. The Bible says that Samuel "ministered before the Lord" (2:11), and that he "continued to grow in stature and in favor with the Lord with men" (2:26).

And then, Hannah, as is often the case after the birth of a first child, other children followed. Although you saw Samuel only once a year after he was weaned, God blessed you with a houseful of children, three more sons and two daughters.

The "why" of suffering is never understood at the time. Looking back, we can see some good that came from Hannah's having to wait for her family. She went to God in her anguish and learned to rely on him for the answer. She understood the preciousness of human life and dedicated her boy to God's service. No doubt her relationships with her other children were sanctified by thankful living. Her daily testimony was, "He settles the barren woman in her home as a happy mother of children. Praise the Lord" (Psalm 113:9).

Praise the Lord, Expectant Mother!

A LITANY OF DEDICATION

Mother: Every good and perfect gift is from above, and coming down from
the Father of the heavenly lights.

Father and Mother: Praise the Lord, O my soul, and forget not all his benefits.

Father: Oh, that my child might live before you.

Mother: For such a child I bless God, in whose bosom he is. May
I and mine become as this little child.

Father: Sons are a heritage from the Lord,
children a reward from him.
Like arrows in the hands of a warrior
are the sons born in one's youth.
Blessed is the man whose quiver
is full of them.

Mother: My soul praises the Lord
and my spirit rejoices in God my Savior,
for he has been mindful of the humble state of his servant.
Bless the Lord, O my Soul.

Father: (Read the following lines, each followed by the words,
"We dedicate this child," spoken together by Mother and Father.)
For bringing joy to our home, reminding
us of the sacredness and preciousness of life,
We dedicate this child.
For teaching us the lessons of humility, love,
and trust,
We dedicate this child,
For furthering your kingdom on earth,
in whatever way he is best qualified,
We dedicate this child.
For your glory, your service, and the
joy of your love and fellowship,
We dedicate this child.

Mother: Good Shepherd, who carries the lambs in your arms, give your Spirit
to us who will be engaged in training the young. Make us patient,
give us tenderness, sincerity, and firmness, and enable us to lead the
young hearts to you, for your name's sake. Amen.[8]

Father: The Lord bless and keep us;
The Lord make his face to shine upon us, and be gracious to us;
The Lord lift up his countenance upon us, and give us peace. Amen.

6. A Life in Our Hands

She dropped in to bring me a thoughtful gift—frozen fruit from her freezer. Although she could not stay long, our conversation turned naturally to our children.

"Our children were born so close together that some of our friends said we didn't know when to stop," she reminisced. "What they didn't know as that each one of our children was prayed for, planned for, and dedicated to God before birth."

Thinking later about this friend's children, all of whom are known as "achievers," I realized that nurture and love had been added to dedication.

A longtime minister related that his mother knelt beneath a tree and dedicated him to the ministry before he was born. We may not want to dedicate our children for something so specific, as we do not know to what Christian vocation they will be best suited. But we do want to "lend them to the Lord," as did Hannah of old. We can trust God to work out the specifics.

On the opposite page is a "Litany of Dedication," to be used for an unborn child. After the baby is here you may wish to have a less formal dedication, including other children in the family and grandparents or other relatives and friends. Many churches have services of dedication for newborn children and their parents. We must remember that we are not simply dedicating the child, but are giving ourselves to God for the nurture and training of that little one.

> *May our sons in their youth*
> *be like plants full grown,*
> *our daughters like corner pillars*
> *cut for the structure of a palace . . . .*
> *Happy the people to whom such*
> *blessings fall!*
> *Happy the people whose God*
> *is the Lord!*

Psalm 144:12, 15, RSV

23

FAITH FOR FATHERS

"A righteous man who walks in his integrity—blessed are
his sons after him!"

Proverbs 20:7, RSV

"As a father has compassion on his children,
so the Lord has compassion on those who fear him"

Psalm 103:13

"Or what man if you, if his son asks him
for bread, will give him a stone?"

Matthew 7:9, RSV

"Fathers, do not exasperate your children;
instead, bring them up in the training and
instruction of the Lord"

Ephesians 6:4.

"I will be a father to you, and you will be my
sons and daughters, says the Lord Almighty . . . ."
"To all who received him, to those who believed in
his name, he gave the right to become children
of God."

2 Corinthians 6:18; John 1:12

7. Husbands Are Pregnant, Too!

Basically, people are much alike when it comes to their needs, hopes, and fears. But how different we are in expressing our joys and problems in the way in which we react to circumstances!

Take, for instance, our friend Alice. Alice in Wonderland, she is, when something exciting comes into her life. Of course, her husband knew all about it the first time she suspected that she was pregnant. After she shared her hopes with him, her mate would have been as disappointed as she if she had been mistaken. In contrast, there is Hilda, carefully reticent until her first trip to the doctor confirms her suspicions. She is the dramatist, one who must set the stage, serve the steak, put on her best negligee, curl up beside the unsuspecting man, and lead up to the Great Announcement.

Women throughout the centuries have had many and varied ways of telling their secret. It is said that in olden times a young wife would begin knitting booties to announce the coming event to her husband.

Probably the most unusual announcement was made by a young woman whose husband left for the Armed Forces overseas before she discovered her pregnancy. Her letters to her beloved began including a bulletin each month, giving her vital measurement statistics. As her figure expanded, her husband caught on! The day came when Baby arrived and statistics were back to normal—or almost, that is!

The book *Husbands and Pregnancy*, by William H. Genne,[9] states that "husbands are pregnant, too!" The author explains in this handbook for fathers-to-be just what is happening within the wife's experience, the development of the baby during each three months of the pregnancy, what to expect during labor and at that momentous time of birth, and what to do when bringing the baby home. The author says, "Despite the obvious physical connection between the mother and baby before it is born, we must not lose sight of this emotional relationship between the husband and wife throughout pregnancy. *The husband is the most important single influence on his wife*. The quality of this emotional relationship is of vital importance to all that is happening."

Preparing for parenthood is a responsibility of both parents-to-be. Pregnancy should be enjoyed together—daily strolls shared when possible, good books read together, emotional problems talked out in a wholesome way. Nowadays there are even classes for couples, where both the husband and the wife are prepared for everything from pinning diapers to cooperating with the doctor at birth. We shouldn't expect all husbands to sit in on the delivery. But how much we need their moral support!

Prayer of a Father-to-Be: "*O Lord, I beg you, let the man of God you sent to us come again to teach us how to bring up the boy who is to be born. . . . What is to be the rule for the boy's life and work?*"—Manoah, father of Samson, recorded in Judges 13:8, 12.

25

SEASONS

I thank Thee for Pain,
the sister of Joy.
I thank Thee for Sorrow,
the twin of Happiness.
Pain, Joy, Sorrow, Happiness.
Four angels at work on the Well of Love.
Pain and Sorrow dig it deep with aches.
Joy and Happiness fill it up with tears
that come with smiles.
For the seasons of emotion in my heart,
I thank Thee, O Lord.[10]

Chandran Devanesen

8. When Love Casts Out Fear

They never called themselves by the name, but they formed a kind of Society-of-the-Apprehensive. Oh, sometimes they were the Society-of-the-Hopeful-Innocents, knitting together while they talked of bassinets, the merits of breast-feeding over bottle, how many diapers were a safe allotment. But often, when husbands weren't listening, they shared their qualms about the birth itself.

They had, of course, read the proper books and soaked up the proper philosophies concerning the forthcoming event. They religiously went through their conditioning exercises, took their walks, and practiced relaxation. But still they wondered. And still they wished it was all over.

Lillian, a charter member of the society (for she it was who first announced she was pregnant), finally took her problem to an older mother who had cheerfully, it seemed, given birth to six.

"Mary, don't you think the Bible is pessimistic about childbirth?" she asked her friend. "God said to Eve, 'With pain you will give birth to children,' and many biblical writers talk of 'pain like that of a woman in labor.' "

"Yes, and then there are Jesus' words: 'A woman giving birth to a child has pain because her time has come; but when her baby is born she forgets the anguish because of her joy that a child is born into the world.' " Mary responded thoughtfully. "And, as I look back, that is just the way it was. Some of my children came easier than others but each of the six experiences was so rewarding, I wouldn't begrudge a single contraction!"

"You know," Mary went on, "we ought to think about what Jesus was trying to say when he used that illustration. He wasn't giving a lecture on 'Facing the Realities of Childbirth.' He was talking about life in a broader perspective. We *do* eliminate fear by knowing what is ahead; confidence and understanding *do* reduce pain-producing tension. But we mustn't expect any worthwhile experience in life to be completely painless—even marriage has its ups and downs.

"The point is that God is with us in all of these moments. That, to quote the apostle Paul, 'suffering produces perserverance; perservance, character; and character, hope.' God's answer, it seems to me, is 'My grace is sufficient for you.' "

> *I sought the Lord, and he answered me; he delivered*
> *   me from all my fears.*
> *Those who look to him are radiant; their faces are never covered with shame.*
> *We wait in hope for the Lord; he is our help and our shield.*
> *In him our hearts rejoice, for we trust in his holy name.*
> *May your unfailing love rest upon us, O Lord,*
> *   even as we put our hope in you.*
>
> **Psalms 34:4-5; 33:20-22**

A MOTHER'S ADDITION TO PSALM 108:1-32

Some went daily about their homely tasks,
washing dishes, making beds, planning balanced meals.
They scrubbed and waxed and ironed white shirts
and sewed on countless buttons.
They saw the hand of the Lord's in the sunrise,
and in the smile on a baby's face.
They heard his voice in questions framed by lips
so lately pressed to the nipple.
They bowed in awe before the promise budding
in young lives entrusted to them.
They trembled at the responsibility the Lord
had laid upon them.

Then they cried to the Lord in their need,
in their emptiness sought satisfaction.
And he delivered them from their distress,
and poured himself into their vacuum.
He sent courage and strength for their duties,
He gave wisdom and grace for their testing.
He tempered their pain with joy,
filled times of communion with sweetness.

Then they rejoiced in his faithfulness,
served him with lips that sang praises;
hands that were kind with his kindness;
feet that were strong with his power.

Let them praise the Lord for his steadfast love,
for his wonderful works to the children of men.
For he answered their cry when they sought him
and met their need with completeness.[11]

Doris E. Schrock

9. Praise for Benefits

A cartoon shows a wife about to be delivered, going up the hospital steps with her husband, who is carrying her suitcase and helping her solicitously. Anxiously, the good man asks, "Are you sure you want to go through with this, dear?"

Obviously, there isn't much choice in the matter at this stage of affairs! But when we do enter the hospital, we are placing ourselves in the hands of competent, skilled, and highly trained specialists. We are paying for the use of a comfortable bed and all kinds of equipment to make the birth of our child safe and our stay as pleasant as possible. It was not always so, even in the days of our mothers, and it is still not the case in many parts of the world.

"Birth," a textbook on obstetrics tells us, "is the complex final act of Nature's greatest miracle—the formation and arrival of a child in the world."[12] The word "obstetrics" comes from the French word *obstetrix*, meaning "midwife." Throughout the centuries, most births were accomplished by midwives, women who passed on their knowledge and their superstitions by word of mouth from generation to generation. In 1513 a book was published in Worms, Germany, entitled *The Garden of Roses for Pregnant Women and Midwives*. This book, which came out in Dutch, German, Latin, French, Spanish, and English, may have been helpful, but was garnished with false teachings, superstitions, and stories of human monsters.

Many advantages which we enjoy today caused hardships for early pioneers in the field of obstetrics. In early times women were never attended by male physicians. One Colonial midwife, Anne Hutchinson of Boston, gave valuable aid at childbirth, but was banished from Massachusetts because of her religious beliefs. Then she was called a witch by superstitious neighbors in Rhode Island, and was finally murdered during Indian raids.

When anesthesia was first used for childbirth, clergymen launched rigorous attacks on the medical profession, using a basis for their protests the words in Genesis 3: "with pain you will give birth to children." Sir James Y. Simpson of England answered this with another quotation from the Bible: "So the Lord God caused the man to fall into a deep sleep." Others pointed out that we can use nature's agents to relieve pain, for what is God-given is to be used by and for mankind.

Gradually, improvements have been made in the care of new babies and their mothers, as obstetrics has become a science, as women's pregnancy has been supervised by able physicians, as false modesty, fear, and ignorance have given to knowledge and understanding. Thus, women no longer die of childbirth fever, and the infant mortality rate has been drastically reduced. Let us be careful not to take for granted God's mercies to us in this privileged land and in this day of enlightenment. Let us thank him for our blessings.

"Praise be to the Lord, to God our Savior, who daily bears our burdens" (Psalm 68:19).

Read Psalm 107:1-32. Then read the "Mother's Addition" to this passage on the opposite page.

FAMILY

"Children's children are a crown to the aged,
and parents are the pride of their children."

Proverbs 17:6

CHILD

The young child, Christ, is straight and wise
And asks questions of the old men, questions
Found under running water for all children,
And found under shadows thrown on still waters
By tall trees looking downward, old and gnarled,
Found to the eyes of children alone, untold,
Singing a low song in the loneliness.
And the young child, Christ, goes on asking
And the old men answer nothing and only know love
For the young child, Christ, straight and wise.[13]

Carl Sandburg

10. A New Shoot on the Family Tree

The mail had brought an unexpected package. Debbie opened it eagerly, finding to her delight a soft-covered baby book. Almost she forgot to fix lunch, so fascinated was she by the pages to be filled. In three weeks? She hoped so.

There was one page, however, which she could begin right now, a drawing of a family tree, with spaces for the names and birth dates of parents, grandparents, even great-great-grandparents. Carefully she printed in the data which she knew by heart from her own side of the family, resolved to see that Jim supplied his ancestry this very evening. What fun!

And then Debbie paused to wonder, once more, what her baby would be like. Jim's dark, penetrating eyes; surely those genes would predominate over her pale green ones. Curls? A bald head? A snub nose? Surely not her freckles, a lifelong plague! Mentally, would the baby be quick like Jim, or slowly pondering everything, like herself? Would he be mechanically minded like her father? Or poetic like Jim's mother? Or always hungry, like her younger brother?

According to the article she had read just this morning, the instant of conception would determine these matters. The baby would be the result of a combination of genes which took place when one of millions of Jim's sperm cells united with a single cell carrying hereditary characteristics from Debbie's ancestry. So many combinations were possible that Debbie wondered how any two children in a family could look alike.

It was fun to imagine presenting her parents with a grandchild, their first. Jim's parents had two already, but they, too, seemed excited about this new baby. To think that she, Debbie, by offering her body as a temporary cradle, could influence the pages of family history, could populate the world with a new citizen, could someday be a grandmother herself!

When we marry, we marry into families. And how fortunate we are to be part of two families in marriage, each enriching our lives and the lives of our children! The psalmist showed the respect which the Hebrew people had for the family tree when he wrote:

> Blessed are all who fear the Lord, who walk in his ways.
> You will eat the fruit of your labor; blessings and prosperity will be yours.

> Your wife will be like a fruitful vine within your house;
> your sons will be like olive shoots around your table.
> Thus is the man blessed who fears the Lord....

> May you live to see your children's children.

> Peace be upon Israel.

Psalm 128:1-4, 6

31

Heartbeats

"Mary treasured up all these things,
and pondered them in her heart."
Luke 2:19

HAIL, MARY

Hail, Mary, full of grace,
The Lord is with thee.
(Uncommon mother. Though birth is commonplace,

This one augured ill, of tragedy, disgrace,
Portent and presage of Gethsemane.)
Hail, Mary, full of grace.

Selected from the human race
To bear God's Child—but privately.
(Uncommon mother! Though birth is commonplace,

You bore this Child in an unlikely space
Where cattle moaned a bleak apostrophe.)
Hail, Mary, full of grace,

Know you the Babe whom you embrace
Is Love—God's grand catastrophe?
(Uncommon mother! Though birth is commonplace,

This one was scandalous—a glorious disgrace
That bound mankind to God in willing slavery.)
Hail, Mary, full of grace,
Uncommon mother—though birth is commonplace.[14]

Jeanne Nuechterlein

34

11. O Favored One!

I feel as though the baby I am carrying will be a great person," an expectant mother confided to a friend.

The feeling she had reminds us of the way all Hebrew mothers felt before the birth of Christ. For, according to the ancient writings of the prophets, some young woman would be honored by bringing into the world the promised Messiah. To whom would God bestow this great honor? No one knew, of course, and so all hoped. And one day, to one least expecting it, the good news came.

Mary, a humble peasant girl, had known love, the love of a noble young man. She looked forward to the role of wife and mother, as any young girl in love and engaged to be married. But she did not expect a visit from a celestial being. No one ever does.

"Greetings to you, Mary. O favored one!—the Lord be with you!"[15]

Mary was frightened, as humans always are when visited by angels. But the angel reassured her.

"Do not be afraid, Mary; God loves you dearly. You are going to be the mother of a son, and you will call him Jesus. He will be great and will be known as the Son of the most high. The Lord God will give him the throne of his forefather, David, and he will be King over the people of Jacob for ever. His reign shall never end."[15]

Mary showed the quality of her character when she asked the question simply, "How can this be? . . . I am not married!"[15]

Obediently and with faith she accepted the explanation of the angel. The Holy Spirit would come upon her and the holy being which would be born would be called the Son of God.

Youthful as she was, probably still a teenager, Mary had strength of body as well as of soul. And it is a good thing, for the days of Mary's pregnancy were unusually taxing. There was the misunderstanding of good Joseph before the angel appeared to him. There was the stigma of the unwed mother. There was the trip (perhaps alone?) to cousin Elizabeth's house, probably a three-day journey. And, when she was heavy with child, there was that long one hundred-mile jaunt over rough roads, on the back of a donkey, to the city of Bethlehem.

For great events we are willing to make great sacrifices. It is the trivial, the petty things which cause us to complain and whine. Mary rose to the occasion, prepared her baby's layette and provisions for the journey, and prayed that the baby would not come before she and Joseph arrived at Bethlehem.

Read carefully the song of Mary from Luke 1:46-55.

Dear God, my soul would also magnify the Lord, and my spirit would rejoice in God my Savior. Help me, your handmaiden, to realize the possibilities which lie dormant in my unborn child. Help me to guide him in serving you effectively. Amen.

35

A MIRACLE

Seems it strange that thou shouldst live forever? Is it less strange that thou shouldst live at all? This is a miracle; and that no more.

Young

Your hands shaped me and made
    me. . . .
Remember that you molded me like
    clay.
    Will you now turn me to dust
      again?
Did you not pour me out like milk
   and curdle me like cheese,
clothe me with skin and flesh
     and knit me together with bones
     and sinews?
You gave me life and showed me
     kindness,
    and in your providence watched
     over my spirit.

Job 10:8-12

36

12. The Babe Leapt for Joy

A humorous picture book for parents-to-be, *Bet It's a Boy,*[16] shows an expectant mother trying to read a book when it suddenly goes flying across the room. Those of us who have felt little feet kick and little arms thrash about within us can identify with that.

It's an exciting day when we feel the first faint movements, as our baby begins to stretch arms and legs. In about the sixth month one feels the baby move around in the "bag of waters," changing positions from side to side, with his head sometimes up and sometimes down. One young wife, who had been married a number of years before she became pregnant, was particularly excited about the signs of life within her, as she wrote to her mother, "Our little one really is starting to kick about these days. I told Bill he moved my arm yesterday and he really laughed and thinks I'm feeling things."

Some of my friends and I were fascinated by a series of color photos in *Life* magazine picturing the growth of the human embryo in various prenatal stages. One picture showed the baby actually in its mother's womb, while the other pictures were of embryos which had been surgically removed for various reasons.

Most of us were surprised to see that the fetus at 18 weeks was sucking its thumb! The article went on to say that the 18-week-old fetus is active and does a great deal of muscle-flexing, as well as going through the motions of crying. The baby opens its eyes for the first time during the seventh month. And all during the time it is developing within the womb, the baby is gaining strength for the day when it will become a visible member of the family, when the umbilical cord, the lifeline for nine months, will be severed and the child will be on its own.

With these facts as a background, Mary's visit to Elizabeth is particularly meaningful. As this very special mother-to-be entered her cousin's house, the older woman cried:

> God's blessing is on you above all women,
> and his blessing on the fruit of your womb.
> Who am I, that the mother of my Lord should visit me?
> I tell you, when your greeting sounded in my ears,
> the baby in my womb leapt for joy.
> How happy is she who has had faith that the Lord's
> promise will be fulfilled!
>
> *Luke 1:42-45*[17]

Prayer of the Jewish Mother at Candlelighting:

> Father of Mercy, continue your loving-kindness to me and
> to my dear ones. Make me worthy to rear my children
> that they walk in the way of the righteous before you,
> loyal to your law and clinging to good deeds. Keep
> from us all manner of shame, grief, and care; and grant
> that peace, light, and joy may ever abide in our home. Amen.

AN ANCIENT PRAYER FOR CHEERFULNESS

O God, animate us to cheerfulness. May we have a joyful sense of our blessings, learn to look on the bright circumstances of our lot, and maintain a perpetual contentedness. Preserve us from despondency and from yielding to dejection. Teach us that nothing can hurt us if, with true loyalty of affection, we keep Thy commandments and take refuge in Thee.[18]

William E. Channing, 1780-1842

*"A happy heart makes the face cheerful . . .
the cheerful heart has a continual feast."*

Proverbs 15:13, 15

13. RX for a Moody Day

We women usually fill the role of chairmen of the Sentiment Department in our homes. It is often we who cry at weddings, shed tears of joy at an unexpected gift, giggle over the comic strips, sense a deep need in our neighbor. God has made many of us that way. Wordsworth says, "Woman, nobly planned, to warn, to comfort, and command."

The men of the family, of course, are not without sentiment, but early training has often conditioned them to be more reticent in displaying their emotions. When it comes to becoming a father, a man has another good reason not to become so emotionalized over the event. It is happening *to* him, but not *within* him. A cartoon reveals this truth, showing the mother-to-be sitting up in bed holding her "middle" while the blissful, expectant father snoozes away in undisturbed slumber. He'll have his chance later—when that 2:00 a.m. bottle needs warming, or Baby develops a case of hiccups which seems to call for his attention! But until the baby arrives in the flesh, fatherhood seems a bit remote to the father-to-be. Of course, there are exceptions. Some young husbands have actually developed "morning sickness" when their wives were pregnant.

A woman psychologist tells us that not a single expectant mother is spared some psychological problems during pregnancy. She lists the most common fears and worries: the coming labor experience, the possibilities of abnormalities in the child, a feeling of being neglected, a fear of being inadequate as a mother, tension with one's own mother coming to the surface, or just a general case of the blues.

Of course, we all have occasional problems even when we aren't pregnant. But during pregnancy changes within our bodies make ordinary problems more acute. One husband, despairing over his wife's moods, wrote to a Christian minister: "My wife is expecting her first baby and her disposition has changed so I hardly know her."

If we accept the fact that we will likely have a few "blue" days, and then also accept our husbands in their humanness and variations of sentimentality, our road will be easier. If possible, pray with your husband for the welfare of the coming child and for strength which comes from reading God's promises. And go ahead and be sentimental, remembering that from the recesses of your heart, the seat of your emotions, will come the very tenderness which will mean life to your child.

> And now, my friends, all that is true,
> All that is noble,
> All that is just and pure,
> All that is lovable and gracious,
> Whatever is excellent and admirable—
> Fill all your thoughts with these things.
> *Philippians 4:8*[19]

BUDS OF PROMISE

Just a bud
Of a blossom,
And yet—
What a promise
Of beauty
Full-blown
And free!

Just a bit
Of a child,
But, oh,
What a vision
Of things
That are
To be![20]

Phyllis C. Michael

14. Double Joy

She still could not believe it was true, not after waiting, hoping, praying for twenty long years. She gazed in the mirror at her own reflection, forgetting to notice her awkward bigness. For she saw only the flushed cheeks and the shining eyes. Joy, joy, joy, was all that she saw in the mirror, was all that she felt, joy mixed with love, almost as fresh as the young love of a dark-haired teenage bride those many years ago.

Why had not God blessed her sooner with fruit of the womb, an heir for her husband, Isaac, while she was still young and strong? Rebekah could not understand the ways of God. And then she thought of Sarah, her mother-in-law, long ago laid to rest in the tomb of Mamre. Sarah had waited much longer for the arrival of Isaac, Rebekah's husband. Isaac had whispered the story in his mother's tent, where Rebekah had learned to know her husband after leaving her own family to become his wife. He had described to her the visit of an angel, announcing that Abraham would have an heir in his old age. He told her of the promise made to Abraham, that his posterity would be as numberless as the sands of the sea and the stars of the sky. Sarah had laughed. She could not believe what she heard.

And now it was Rebekah's turn to be shocked by a joy too great to describe. And the joy was double! After all that waiting—twins! She had suspected as much by the activity which she felt in her womb, by her tremendous size. Remembering that God had spoken directly to Father Abraham, that he had sent a messenger to announce the birth of Isaac, Rebekah had inquired of the Lord what she felt going on within her. And God had answered.

"Two nations are in your womb," he had said, "and two peoples from within you will be separated; one people will be stronger than the other, and the older will serve the younger." The story in Genesis 25 goes on to describe the birth of the twins, how Esau was born first and how Jacob symbolically took hold of his brother's heel. So different were they in physical appearance and emotional makeup!

Twins always present a certain kind of problem for parents. One can make a double formula, one mother of twins points out, but two babies cannot be "bubbled" or diapered simultaneously. And, especially if they are identical, there is the problem of helping them to become individuals and to grow in their own right.

Rebekah did not have a copy of Dr. Spock's helpful manual or a pediatrician to give her advice. She and Isaac, although they were very much in love, were unwise in their show of favoritism for the boys. If only Rebekah had loved equally and well those sons of different natures, if only she had placed their futures in the hands of God! But like so many of us, she tried to shape the destiny of her boy Jacob, forgetting that God had her family and their posterity in his almighty hand.

Father God, our job is to love, to train, to exhort, to guide, to pray. Beyond that our unborn child is yours. We know that you fashioned this delightful person and that you have a plan for our child's life. Help us to remember that the carrying out of this plan is the work of your Spirit. Amen.

41

BIRTH

Just when each bud was big with bloom,
And as prophetic of perfume,
When spring, with her bright horoscope,
Was sweet as an unuttered hope;

Just when the last star flickered out,
And twilight, like a soul in doubt,
Hovered between the dark and dawn,
And day lay waiting to be born;

Just when the gray and dewy air
Grew sacred as an unvoiced prayer,
And somewhere through the dusk she heard
The stirring of a nested bird—

Four angels glorified the place:
Wan Pain unveiled her awful face;
Joy, soaring, sang; Love, brooding, smiled;
Peace laid upon her breast a child.[21]

Annie R. Stillman (Grace Raymond)

42

15. If You Want a Thing Well Done

She didn't really think that she would need the information. But Mary Louise (her real name)[22] believed in being prepared. So she read carefully what one would do if she found it necessary to deliver her own baby. The thought did not terrify her, for the coming of babies had been fairly simple and exhilarating for this young woman.

It had all started with Baby No. 1. Someone had introduced Mary Louise to the book by Dr. Grantly Read, *Childbirth Without Fear*.[23] She had conscientiously done her exercises and learned to relax. Young and strong, without complications, Mary Louise had watched her baby's birth in a mirror. The second birth had been no more complicated, and Mary Louise looked forward to her third.

Yes, she was glad she had read about delivering babies. For one Sunday morning things began happening fast. By the time husband, Paul, had showered the children and put them in the car to go to Grandmother's, Mary Louise knew that she would never make it to the hospital in time. And by the time Paul got the doctor on the phone, so excited that he forgot to give his name, the doctor heard the baby crying in the background. "Your baby is already there," the doctor told him.

"I was way up in the clouds emotionally," Mary Louise says. "It was wonderful. First, I looked her over from top to bottom and turned her all around. Then I loved her and loved her and loved her. I have never felt so fulfilled! Truly, it was the best day of my life. There was no one to interfere with our joy—Paul's and mine—just the two of us, rejoicing in our own and God's creation. And I think that all that love, right at the beginning of her life, contributed to making our Mary Sue such a good baby."

Mary Louise knows, of course, that she was fortunate in her deliveries, but she ended by saying, "I feel sorry for girls who look ahead to the experience of birth with fear, dreading it, when they could be helped to enjoy the experience."

A Thought to Ponder: "Can a woman forget the baby at her breast and have no compassion on the child she has borne?" . . . "Perfect love drives out fear." . . . "As a mother comforts her child, so will I comfort you."

O heavenly Father, thank you for the joyful experience to which I look forward, the fulfillment of my dreams, the birth of our new baby. Make that special day, I pray, a hallowed one for the baby's father and myself, as we put our trust in you. Amen.

A PRAYER FOR ALL GOD'S CHILDREN

O God, since Thou has laid the little children into our arms in utter helplessness, with no protection save our love, we pray that the sweet appeal of their baby hands may not be in vain.

Let no innocent life in our cities be quenched again in useless pain through our ignorance and sin.

May we who are mothers and fathers seek eagerly to join wisdom to our love, lest love itself be deadly when unguided by knowledge.

Bless the doctors and nurses, and all the friends of men who are giving of their skill and devotion to the care of our children.

If there are any who were kissed by love in their own infancy, but who have no child to whom they may give as they have received, grant them such largeness of sympathy that they may rejoice to pay their debt in full to all children who have need of them.

Forgive us, our Father, for the heartlessness of the past. Grant us great tenderness for all babes who suffer, and a growing sense of the divine mystery that is brooding in the soul of every child; for the sake of Jesus Christ our Savior. Amen.[24]

W. Rauschenbach, 1912

16. Jesus and the Babies

The Nameless Ones'! Through the pages of holy history they walk; women deprived of the most personal identification human beings can have—their own names. In the biblical story they are identified as 'a certain woman,' 'a woman that was a sinner,' 'the women that were with him,' 'a widow,' 'a great woman,' the wife of this man, the daughter of that, the mother-in-law of another. Does the absence of a name mean that their significance was slight? Does it blur their faces and impersonalize their lives?"

Thus writes Miriam Sieber Lind in a play called "The Nameless Ones." Then she introduces to us a procession of women in the Bible who have contributed to our lives but who were unnamed in the Scriptures. She goes on to tell us this story:

> "And they were bringing children to him, that he might touch them; and the disciples rebuked them. But when Jesus saw it he was indignant, and said to them, 'Let the children come to me, do not hinder them; for to such belongs the kingdom of God. Truly, I say to you, whoever does not receive the kingdom of God like a child shall not enter it.' And he took them in his arms and blessed them, laying his hands upon them."

> ### Mark 10:13-16, RSV

" 'They' brought unto him infants and children. Who would 'they' be? Who but the mothers of the children! Who else would care enough about having their children receive the touch of our Lord, care enough to flaunt the hostile stares and words of those self-chosen body guards who thought they knew Jesus? They didn't know him, in some ways, as well as those mothers who intuitively brought to him the most precious things in their lives—their children.

"And you, Nameless Mother, you began with your children a procession which has never stopped. Through all time since, all over the world, the line still forms . . . mothers bringing to Jesus their children for his blessing. And somehow, they all seem to understand that it is not so much a matter of a magical touch upon the child, as a sort of magical touch upon the child, as a sort of dedication of the mother herself.

"We salute you who had the courage to come to Jesus with our children, and to receive from him those wonderful words which not only have welcomed both mothers and children ever since, but which weighted the worth of a child, and which brought us all a step nearer to the kingdom of heaven."[25]

SOME MODERN PRAYERS

Good-night, Lord;
I'm very tired,
But you were, too.

Can't say much,
But you know all;
Even that I'm yawning.

Good-night, Lord,
Secure my sleep;
See you in the morning.

                —C.H.

"O Lord, help me to understand that you ain't gwine to let nuthin' come my way that you and me together can't handle." [26]

17. Good for What Ails You!

A nurse, working in the famous Lying-in-Hospital in Boston, still chuckles over a patient who was in labor and who was having difficulty concentrating on everything which was going on. A doctor had just been in to examine her and the nurse wondered what the doctor had said.

"I'm not quite sure," the patient responded weakly, "It sounded like 'e pluribus unum' to me."

In one large hospital there was a nurse who seemed like a guardian angel to maternity patients. When she came on duty, the patient knew that all her questions would be kindly and patiently answered. And as the contractions came close together and the delivery room was obviously the next destination, this nurse would call out, "Bring the chariot!"

How helpful a splash of humor can be to ease the stresses of life! There is good evidence that Jesus exercised his sense of humor when dealing with people and their problems. Little children would not have been drawn to a man of dour expression and sour outlook on life.

Some mothers-to-be have actually taken joke books into the labor room, though most of us would have some trouble concentrating, even on a good joke, in the last stages of labor! But all through our pregnancy our attitudes toward the various stages, inconveniences, and annoyances can be salted with humor if we determine to cultivate a happy frame of mind. And this attitude will go along to the hospital with us, right alongside the ruffly gown and shiny new baby book.

One mother, in looking back over her pregnancy, remarked, "I found myself becoming too self-centered and introspective, and increasingly recognized the need to center my thoughts on God." The joy of the Lord—what an antidote for those feelings of self-pity or inadequacy which sometimes overtake us! The psalmist put it this way:

You have made known to me the path of life; you will fill me with joy in your presence.

Psalm 16:11

And the writer of the Proverbs prescribed laughter as the best medicine when he said:

A cheerful heart is good medicine, but a downcast spirit dries up the bones.

Proverbs 17:22, RSV

SONG FOR A FIFTH CHILD

Mother, O mother, come shake out your cloth!
Empty the dustpan, poison the moth,
Hang out the washing and butter the bread,
Sew on a button and make up a bed.
    Where is the mother whose house is so shocking?
    She's up in the nursery, blissfully rocking!

Oh, I've grown as shiftless as Little Boy Blue
    (Lullaby, rockaby, lullaby loo).
Dishes are waiting and bills are past due
    (Pat-a-cake, darling, and peek, peekaboo).
The shopping's not done and there's nothing for stew
And out in the yard there's a hullabaloo
But I'm playing Kanga and this is my Roo.
Look! Aren't her eyes the most wonderful hue?
    Lullaby, rockaby, lullaby loo.)

Oh, cleaning and scrubbing will wait till tomorrow,
But children grow up, as I've learned to my sorrow.
So quiet down, cobwebs. Dust, go to sleep.
I'm rocking my baby. Babies don't keep.[27]

Ruth Hulburt Hamilton

48

18. A Family Affair

There is, in the Bible, a beautiful story of an older child's love and concern for a baby brother. It is the story of Miriam, the little girl who hid to watch a baby whose life was in danger.

Tiny Moses and his people lived in a land where they slaved for a nation which did not appreciate them. Pharaoh, the ruling monarch, was uneasy about this transplanted people who were multiplying so fast in his country. Thus he ordered all Israelite baby boys murdered upon birth.

Moses, destined to lead his people from their place of bondage back to their native land, was three months old when his mother and big sister contrived a plan to save his life. After placing the baby in a basket on the bank of the Nile River, Jochebed stationed Miriam close by as the daughter of Pharaoh came on the scene. When this gentle woman took pity on the baby and decided to adopt him for herself, Miriam was there to suggest a Hebrew nurse to care for him. Of course, this nurse was the baby's own mother.

A modern mother was equally successful in making the coming of a new baby a family affair. This family tackled "projects" from time to time. Perhaps it was the laying of a new patio, stone by stone, or the forming of a family orchestra. "The baby," she wrote in a letter to a friend, "is our 'family project' this year."

A member of a family of twelve children recalls that even when she was in her teens, she did not resent it when her mother announced that another child was on the way. "We always hoped it would be twins," she smiles.

The coming of a new member to a family should increase its sense of togetherness. There will be adjustments for both younger and older children, and depending upon their age, there will be various ways of announcing the event to them. It is not wise to tell a young child too long ahead of time, for it is hard at such an age to wait. Of course, mothers nowadays don't perpetuate the stork myth, but try to explain the miracle of birth honestly in simple words. It is important that a baby never comes as surprise, even to the smallest child.

We must expect adjustments and take in stride natural feelings of jealousy in children who have up to now been the center of their parents' universe. Letting the child help get ready for the baby and later help with its care, telling stories of their own babyhood days, and reassuring them by giving them extra time and attention—these things are important in the emotional care of sister or brother. And the older the children, the more they may be involved in plans and preparations for the Big Event.

O God, our Father, we give thanks for the child we are expecting; help us to live together as a family in love, joy, and peace; give us wisdom to be good parents, that we may all love and serve you faithfully; through Jesus Christ our Lord. Amen.[28]

AN EXPECTANT MOTHER'S PRAYER

Heavenly Father, I am about to go seeking a little soul, a thing that shall be mine as no other thing in the whole world has been mine.

Bring me through my hour strong and well for the sake of my baby. Prepare me for real motherhood. Preserve my mind from all doubts and worry, and take all fear-misgivings from me so that the little mind that is forming may become a brave, clean battler in the world of dangers. . . . And, God, when the child lies in my arms and draws its life from me, and when those eyes look up to mine to learn what this new world is like, I pledge Thee, the child shall find reverence in me, and no fear; truth and no shame; love, strong as life and death; no hates.

O God, make my baby love me. I ask no endowments of excellencies for my child, but only that the place of motherhood, once given me, may never be taken from me. As long as the soul lives that I shall bring forth, let there be in it one secret shrine that all always be mother's.

Give it a clean mind and a warm free soul. And I promise Thee that I shall study the little one to find what gifts and graces Thou hast implanted that I may develop them.

I shall respect its personality. And now, Father, I fold my hands and place them between Thy hands and pray, in Jesus' name, that it may be Thy will to give me a normal baby, and make me a normal mother. Amen.[29]

19. Are You Superstitious?

Grandma was a midwife. Living in the mountains of Virginia, she could be depended upon to help whenever she was needed. Her family, consisting of Grandpa, five girls, and two boys, was never surprised to find that Mama had saddled her horse or walked to a neighboring farm where a new baby was expected. Common sense and skillful hands went a long way. And Grandma had her almanac. She knew when her first grandchild could be expected, even though that grandchild was tardy, for babies put in their appearance in the full of the moon.

Many of Grandma's ideas, handed down to her from previous generations, were filled with superstition. She would not allow a mother-to-be to walk through a fish market, for fear that the unborn would be "marked" with a birthmark in the shape of a fish. But her idea about the moon wasn't so far off. In one large city hospital it was observed that during the time of months when the moon comes out in all its glory, the maternity ward was usually filled to overflowing!

Throughout the centuries many superstitions and tales of folklore about childbirth have been handed down from mother to daughter, or in some cases from father to daughter. There is, for instance, the notion that February is a good month to be born if you want to be intelligent (like Washington and Lincoln). One father warned his daughter not to touch any part of her body if she suddenly received a shock of any kind. For her unborn child would be marked in that very spot! The father documented his warning by telling of a pregnant mother who was frightened by a snake and touched her stomach. When the baby was born, a birthmark in the form of a snake was on its stomach.

A pastor, shepherding a Spanish-American church in a large city, recalls that one of his members walked many blocks to buy a piece of watermelon for the pastor's pregnant wife. In this gentleman's background it was considered harmful to the baby to allow a pregnant mother to have an unfulfilled craving.

Many such beliefs are harmless, but in our scientific age we want to know the truth. And truth is best obtained from reliable sources, such as our doctors, informative books, good magazines. A mother may worry, for instance, that she has harmed her baby because of an unexpected shock or fright. A frank discussion with her physician will put her mind at ease.

The apostle Paul, in writing to his young friend Timothy, had been praising Timothy's mother and grandmother, both of whom were wise and good women, responsible for the high character of the son. Paul tells Timothy to "fan into flame the gift of God, which is in you. . . ." And then comes the thought which speaks to our need as young mothers: "For God did not give us a spirit of timidity, but a spirit of power, of love and of self-discipline" (2 Timothy 1:7).

This is all the equipment we need for a happy pregnancy!

51

HE IS THE ONE

"Then the Lord said, 'Rise and anoint him; he is the one.'"

1 Samuel 16:12

GOD'S CHOSEN KING

He was Jesse's youngest son—
A comely boy, and fair,
Yet brave and strong.
Untrampled by the heavy tread of Time
His life was on the Open—free, sublime—
Within his gentle soul he held the lilt of Spring,
And to the music of his harp-strings—loved to sing
In verse and song, the praises of his heavenly King.
He felt the hand of God within his own,
And tempted even death—stout-hearted and alone—
And knew the victory won
Ere the struggle had begun—
God's hand within his own—free, brave and strong.[30]

Lola F. Echard

20. *God Looks on the Heart*

The nicest compliment parents can receive is when someone says something good about one of their children. I have watched the eyes of a mother light up as a friend remarked about the wholesome attitudes of her teenage daughter. When a child receives an award, a scholarship, or simply a word of commendation, parental pride goes into orbit.

But what would it be like to hear God give special recognition to one of our children? This happened when the Lord sent the prophet Samuel to the house of Jesse to anoint a king. As the oldest son passed before Samuel, God whispered in his ear that this was not the chosen one. God said,

> "Do not consider his appearance or his height.... The Lord does not look at the things man looks at. Man looks at the outward appearance, but the Lord looks at the heart."

Eliab must have been a good-looking fellow, for Samuel would have anointed him, had not God told him otherwise. As each of the next six sons passed before Samuel, God indicated to the prophet that he was not the one. Finally, Samuel asked Jesse if these were all the sons he had. David was outside taking care of the sheep.

Good looks are usually not a handicap; indeed, they can be a real asset. But there is an inner quality, a condition of heart, which God sees when he looks for leadership. When the young man David was brought before Samuel, God told Samuel that this was the one, the one whom he would later describe as a "man after my own heart." A handsome boy with striking physical features, David also commanded respect for his pleasing personality and stalwart character. After his anointing "from that day on the Spirit of the Lord came upon David in power."

How do we build character in a child? Fourteen top Boy Scouts were asked what their parents gave them which meant the most in their growing-up years."

"Love," one boy said, "is the greatest gift a parent can give."

"Trust," responded a boy from Massachusetts. "They didn't announce one night, 'Donald, we trust you,' but they conveyed a feeling of trust in me through their own actions over the years of my childhood."

"Faith," said a Scout from the state of Washington. "It gave my life a purpose."

Another boy thanked his parents for teaching him to be honest and responsible. "I say this," he said, "because I feel that these basic moral beliefs are the backbone of all life and a foundation for living."

"Standards," replied a boy from Iowa. "If the parents set good examples and good rules a child has jumped over one of the biggest stumbling blocks in his life."

To grow up at one's best every child has basic needs which a parent can provide: love, acceptance, security, protection, independence, faith, guidance, and control.[32] Your baby will no doubt receive many gifts, but your child will treasure most the gift of love.

Great Expectations

"Mary . . . being great with child."
Luke 2:5, KJV

REST

"I will lie down and sleep."

Psalm 4:8

NIGHT

Lord, I thank Thee for night,
the time of cool and quiet,
the time of sweet and enchantment
when a deep mystery pervades everything.
The time when soul speaks to soul in common desire
to partake of the hush of the ineffable.
The time when the moon and the stars
speak to man of his high calling and destiny.
The time of repose and calm
when the fever of the mind subsides
and uncertainty gives place
to the sense of eternal purpose.
O Lord, I thank Thee for night.[33]

Chandran Devanesen

21. Take Care of Yourself!

Take care of yourself! Take care of that baby!" A mother-to-be often receives these words of advice, given lightly or seriously, by well-meaning friends and relatives. Fortunately, in our world of medical know-how it is possible to take care of oneself and of one's unborn child without strain or anxiety.

We know that regular checkups by our doctor are important. Many doctors supply their patients with little books of information, and the wise mother-to-be will visit her community library for more help. Where parents' classes are available, expectant parents ask questions and get a better understanding of the birth process.

We know, too, that it is vital that we eat properly, balancing our diet with lean meats or other proteins, vegetables, cereals, and milk, and avoiding rich and fatty foods. There was a day when a mother was told that she was "eating for two." But alas, although our child's well-being depends on what we eat, it doesn't mean that we double our calories!

One mother wrote an article in which she described how she gained an inordinate amount of weight with two pregnancies, then analyzed her reasons for overeating, mending her ways with her third child. As a doctor's wife she knew that her weight was putting extra burden on her heart and kidneys, causing varicose veins, rocketing her blood pressure, making her feel awkward and awful, and causing embarrassment to her husband. After self-scrutiny with the help of a specialist, she realized that she was overeating because of unconscious emotional needs, compensating for frustrations by going to the refrigerator.

Many mothers-to-be are chronically tired. According to one authority[34] the reasons for fatigue are not all known, but during the first few months are related to changes in body chemistry and in the last months to "the burden of carrying a fluid-filled womb and an active fetus." Catnaps may be the order of the day for some women, and surely all will need a good night's sleep. Dr. Keith P. Russel suggests two periods of daytime rest—one half hour to forty-five minutes in the morning, and twice that amount in the afternoon. He also suggests ways of preventing overfatigue.

This does not mean, of course, that we avoid exercise in order to avoid fatigue. Dr. Frederick W. Goodrich, Jr., in his book, *Preparing for Childbirth*,[35] has an excellent chapter on developing good muscle tone through proper exercises, as well as a chapter on relaxation techniques.

It isn't easy to slow down our pace of living, but we don't need to feel guilty when we "take care of ourselves" by getting sufficient rest when drowsy, by eating the right kind of foods, by keeping up our morale with recreation or an evening out. For the Lord will soon renew our strength and reward us for our patience.

"Lift Thou up our eyes, that we may behold him that spreadeth out the heavens: the Holy One, the everlasting God. So wilt Thou renew our strength; and in the coming days we shall mount up with wings as eagles, we shall run and not be weary, we shall walk and not faint. Glory be to Thee, O Lord, Most High!"[36]

EVERYMAID

King's Daughter!
Wouldst thou be all fair,
Without—within—
Peerless and beautiful,
A very queen?

Know then—
Not as men build unto the Silent One—
With clang and clamor,
Traffic of rude voices,
Clink of steel on stone,
And din of hammer—
Not so the temple of thy grace is reared.
But—in the inmost shrine
Must thou begin,
And build with care
A Holy Place,
A place unseen,
Each stone a prayer.
Then, having built,
Thy shrine sweep bare
Of self and sin,
And all that might demean;
And, with endeavor,
Watching ever, praying ever,
Keep it fragrant—sweet, and clean:
So by God's grace, it be fit place—
His Christ shall enter and shall dwell therein
Not as in earthly fane—where chase
Of steel and stone may strive to win
Some outward grace—
Thy temple face is chiselled from within.[37]

John Oxenham

22. That Maternal Glow

The subject came up at a neighborhood coffee hour. Rachel, sporting a new and becoming maternity dress, was collecting compliments from her friends. "Frankly," she admitted, "I could hardly wait to put on this dress. It is sort of a badge of honor with me, telling my friends the good news!"

"I wish I felt that way about it," Donna replied. "Somehow or other I feel more awkward all the time. Every time I look in a full-length mirror, I want to run and hide. Even Bill had had a time getting used to my shape! You should have heard what the neighbor boy said, 'Boy, are you big! When is that baby coming?'"

Everyone laughed, but Mabel topped it all when she told of how little Dickie had embarrassed her when she was pregnant the second time. Going up to the supermarket butcher, a man with a Santa Claus build, he had asked innocently, "Are you pregnant, too?"

It is small wonder that expectant mothers worry about their appearance, with all the daily propaganda on keeping husbands with the aid of everything from hair tints to breath pills. One movie star, tired of being admired for outward attributes, sighed, "If only they would care about the inside 'me'!"

It helps to remember that our expanding shape is a temporary condition. And it is comforting to realize that true beauty comes from an inner radiance which is produced by happiness. Joy, plus increased metabolism in pregnancy, often gives the pregnant wife what is known as the "maternal glow." The awareness that a new person is being formed within her and the anticipation of the momentous event to come add to the inner glow of the mother-to-be.

Several writers in the New Testament pointed out to Christian women that true adornment should come from inside. Paul writes: "And the women should be the same way [free from sin and anger and resentment], quiet and sensible in manner and clothing. Christian women should be noticed for being kind and good, not for the way they fix their hair or because of their jewels or fancy clothes" (1 Timothy 2:9-10).[38]

And Peter says: "Don't be concerned about the outward beauty that depends on jewelry, or beautiful clothes, or hair arrangement. Be beautiful inside, in your hearts, with the lasting charm of a gentle and quiet spirit which is so precious to God" (1 Peter 3:3-4).[38]

Suitable, comfortable, and pretty clothes, good personal hygiene, shining, clean hair—these all boost the morale and contribute to a woman's well-being during pregnancy. But, as at other times, enthusiasm for life, a kind and outgoing spirit, and peace with God and oneself are beauty aids you can't buy at the drugstore!

Lord Jesus, we come to Thee now as little children. Dress us again in clean pinafores; make us tidy once more with the tidiness of true remorse and confession. O, wash our hearts, that they may be clean again. Make us to know the strengthening joys of the Spirit, and the newness of life which only Thou canst give. Amen.[39]

CALLED OF GOD

"Before I was born the Lord called me;
from my birth he has made mention of my name."

Isaiah 49:1

FOR JAMES

Saint James the Less,
We pray thee, bless
Young James' childhood days:
And, prithee, later
Saint James the Greater,
Conduct him through life's tortuous ways:
Then, less and greater, he shall bring
Smiles for our frowns, hope for our suffering.[40]

B. C. Boulter
(lines written for the baptism of James Piercy, grandson of Lord Piercy)

23. What's in a Name?

Now, isn't that just like a kid brother?" Phyllis looked up from her letter with a chuckle. "He sent me a list of boys' names to choose from, and here they are: Casper, Ichabod, Bartholomew, Alphanso, and Ferdinand. Quite a sense of humor, that boy!"

"But you know," Phyllis' friend mused, "I know people who have saddled children with names that are just as bad. It doesn't seem fair to the child to hang a tag on him that he'll hate all his life. And I know other people, whom I admire, who name their children only Bible names, like Matthew, Elizabeth, or Timothy. Do you think a name affects the child's feeling toward himself?"

In Bible times people thought more about the meaning of names than they do today, often giving a child a name which they hoped would express his personality and character. The mother often named the baby, although sometimes the father chose the name. In the case of John the Baptist, the relatives apparently expected him to be named after someone in the family, for they were surprised when the father insisted that "his name is John."

Judas is a solemn example of one who brought joy to his home when he was born but did discredit to his name in later years. For "Judas" means "thanksgiving" or "praise to God." On the other hand, Jacob, who most of his life had a name which means "supplanter" or "cheat," lived up to his name until God changed him and changed his name, as well. After his conversion God gave him the name "Israel," which means "prince." As the prince of his race, he passed on the name "Israel" to a nation.

Bruce Larson, in an article entitled "Whom Do You Want to Be?"[41] points out that "we become what we are called." If our name, in our own mind, is Timid, or Dishonest, or Self-Conscious, or Fearful, or Indifferent, or Reserved, that is the way we look at ourself. At the same time, in God's sight, our name might be Courageous, or Wonderful, or Faithful, or Bountiful, or Warm, or Generous. Larson says that we also determine what others become, by the way we think of them, and what we expect from them. Particularly is this true of our relationship to our children.

So it doesn't matter so much what you name your baby—Ruth, or Shirley, or Tom, or Kirk. What does matter is how you feel toward that child. Do you see the infant as a child of God, a beloved person, an individual capable of making a unique contribution to his world?

Jesus saw Simon Peter's possibilities, despite Peter's many blunderings, when he said, "So you are Simon the son of John? You shall be called Cephas (which means Peter)" (John 1:42, RSV). We know that Peter means "rock" and that Peter became a pillar in the early church, a strong and solid character, fulfilling Jesus' expectations of him.

WELCOMING THE CHILD

God, who hast given to us the privilege of calling Thee by the precious name of Father, we thank Thee again for this blessing as we welcome a child to share the earthly pilgrimage of family and friends. Please extend to this child a long and happy lifetime to explore and enjoy the bounties of this, Thy wonderful world.

May the helplessness of this new life depending upon earthly parents remind all of us in the adult world of our own need to rely on Thee. Forgive us for the times when we have forgotten that Thou art our heavenly Father, more eager to help than we are to ask.

Keep us as little children, looking to Thee daily to give us wisdom and strength to meet the changing needs of our lives, even as we place this child into Thy loving protection. Amen.[42]

Ruth C. Ikerman

AN INFANT

But what am I?
An infant crying in the night:
An infant crying for the light;
And with no language but a cry.[43]

Alfred Lord Tennyson

24. This Brave New World

Today your baby rests securely "beneath your heart," as the old saying goes, getting ready for the day when he or she will become a part of our world.

You are looking forward to that event with mixed feelings. But if you think birth is a traumatic experience for a mother, think what it must be like for the newborn.

Besides becoming accustomed to a drop in temperature, a dry world instead of a wet one, light instead of darkness, and breathing as a way of getting oxygen, the newborn's heart and circulatory apparatus must also make drastic adjustments.

"The harsh experience of birth is a great strain on the baby, climaxed by dramatic changes in his bodily functions and in his environment. From his dark, protected, effortless existence, he is thrust into a world of light and noise, air that envelopes his skin and rushes into his lungs. Even soft clothing and his weight against a surface are strange sensations...."[44]

How can we as mothers best help our baby get used to this "brave new world"?

One good way of making the baby feel at home in the world is breast-feeding, a deeply satisfying experience for mother and child. In "The Wondrous World of the Newborn"[45] Dr. Margaret Liley and Beth Day write: "It takes the newborn baby several days to recover from the experience of birth and feel hungry. Usually, his first hunger pangs coincide with the time when his mother's milk is available: about the third day. One of the reasons breast-feeding is so strongly recommended is that it provides reassurance; the baby needs the nearness of another human body, the gentle monotony of the heartbeat, the warmth of adult arms."

A newborn baby is tired for the first weeks of life and wants mostly to sleep and eat. Dr. Lily goes on to point out, "Accustomed to the relative weightlessness of the womb, he finds the effort to compete with gravity to be quite considerable. Baths are pleasurable to him because the buoyancy of the water gives him a brief respite from the constant pull of gravity."

The very helplessness of a tiny baby usually inspires mother love to cuddle and caress and speak in tender tones. Every mother should own a rocking chair, not only to fulfill the baby's early needs for rhythmic motion, but to comfort and soothe the growing child. She may not have the voice of a nightingale, but her crooning will be appreciated by her audience of one. Probably never again will she be so completely accepted as in this wonderful "rocking-chair stage" of the mother-child relationship.

Babies do not understand English! Nor Arabic! Nor Chinese! But they respond to the language of love as revealed through their senses. Johnson and Johnson, famed makers of baby products, have a nice way of saying it: "Love is something I can feel. That's Mommy's hand, I know, because I can feel the gentleness in it. Mommy's hand feels better than anything. It feels like love."[46]

"Thou hast made children and babes at the breast sound aloud thy praise" (Matthew 21:16).[47]

A PRAYER FOR FAITH

Our Father, give us the faith to believe that it is possible for us to live victoriously even in the midst of dangerous opportunity that we call crisis. Help us to see that there is something better than patient endurance or keeping a stiff upper lip, and that whistling in the dark is not really bravery.

Trusting in Thee, may we have the faith that goes singing in the rain, knowing that all things work together for good to them that love Thee. Through Jesus Christ, our Lord. Amen.[48]

"Make that possible to me, O Lord, by grace, which appears impossible to me by nature"

Thomas à Kempis

25. Welcome, Baby!

Welcome to the greatest adventure in a woman's life." Thus begins an excellent book entitled *Adventure to Motherhood*.[49] "But beware, you who travel this road. Most adventures are beset with peril. Travel this road at your own risk! Have you ever read an adventure story without suspense, intrigue, and struggle?"

For most of us, the coming baby is a welcome addition to the family. But before we put out the welcome mat, let's assess our situation realistically. For if we aren't aware of motherhood's struggles, we may be disillusioned.

To begin with, we bring to this experience a limited amount of energy and a body which is still undergoing physiological changes. It will be at least six weeks until we are operating at full capacity. In the meantime we must make numerous adjustments in our day's schedule, keeping the baby happy, other members of the family reassured, and ourselves in a reasonably level-headed condition. There may be formulas to prepare (a pokey business, at best), endless laundry (newborn babies are always wet), a shift of household furnishings to make room for the newest member, and constant peeking into the baby book to be sure we are doing everything right. Add to this the fact that no one has informed this little creature that people eat three times a day! The alarm in this tiny mechanism goes off at irregular intervals ranging from two to four hours, and at the ungodly hour of 2:00 a.m.

Several women, who are really good mothers at heart, were asked what things were hardest for them to get used to in being a mother. "I never thought that, loving my son as I do, I could become irritated at him," one honest mother confessed. "Adjusting my real baby to the ideas I received from reading books," another added. "Feeling that I am shut out of my husband's world," "Staying home with the children," and "All the noise and confusion" were also mentioned. One young woman, always hungry, confessed that she found it hard to wait until her children's needs were met!

A new mother struggled with resentment toward the 2:00 a.m. feeding, until she ran across an article which suggested making good use of this time. "These rendezvous with nighttime can be a time when one is alone with the baby without the interference of siblings, the ringing phone, or the doorbell," she wrote. Then, before returning to bed, she learned to relax and enjoy the special things of night, the stars or the falling snow. In the kitchen she indulged in a glass of cold milk or a piece of cake saved from supper. Funny thing about it was that when she thus improved her attitude, the baby dropped the night feeding!

Motherhood is an adventure in more ways than one. Perhaps its greatest challenge is selflessness. Jesus said, "Whoever loses his life for my sake will find it" (Matthew 10:39).

MOTHER, I'M COMING!"

I hear you, Sweet! And I'll prepare
So lovingly your dainty wear.
Oh, I will dream and scheme each day;
And, planning, put the pennies away.
Then, too, not only will I make
Soft woolly comforts for your sake;
But I will fashion if I can,
Fine raiment for your inner man.
I will not think on evil things
Lest I should clip my darling's wings.
I'll set my heart to understand
The great salvation God has planned.
Yes, every atom of my being,
All feeling, tasting, hearing, seeing,
He shall refine, and garnish, too.
I'll be God's woman through and through.
Lord, take me; and, if this may be,
Possess my little child through me.[50]

26. All Kinds of Mothers

In 1963 a collection of great paintings on the subject of mother and child was organized by the American Federation of Arts. Richard L. Gelb writes about this exhibit, "Of all the possible subjects upon which the artist can draw for inspiration, none has more universal appeal than that of mother and child." From this art exhibit came a book, *Mother and Child in Modern Art.*[51]

As we browse through this interesting collection, we can see that motherhood takes many forms. Not a single mother is exactly like another mother. This can be a consolation for those of us who are afraid we won't "measure up." And the best thing about it is that our child will like our particular brand of motherhood and will think it is the greatest!

Of course, we can improve the quality of our motherhood by a little study, even though our personalities and abilities will influence the way in which we give ourselves to our children. Reading Dr. Frances Ilg's comments on the paintings of mothers and children, we see that some mothers are possessive, while others allow a fine balance of "relatedness" and "separateness." Some mothers expect children to be miniature adults, while others know how to play with their children and how to see things through the eyes of a child. Some mothers resent their children, while others are emotionally prepared to give wholesome and intelligent love.

How important is the quality of a mother's life to the quality of person her child will become! This is illustrated time and again in the Old Testament stories of the kings of Israel. A biography will begin, "His mother's name was . . ." and he did "that which was right in the sight of the Lord." Or conversely, "His mother's name was . . ." and "He too walked in the ways of the house of Ahab, for his mother encouraged him in doing wrong."

Well has it been said, "The mother's heart is the child's schoolroom."

Dear God, in spite of my many faults and human limitations, help me to be the best kind of mother to my child, remembering to be myself, yet allowing you to make that self in your own image. Amen.

BOY OR GIRL?

Some folks pray for a boy, and some
For a golden-haired little girl to come.
    Some claim to think there is more of joy
    Wrapped up in the smile of a little boy,
    While others pretend that the silky curls
    And plump, pink cheeks of the little girls
    Bring more of bliss to the old homeplace
    Than a small boy's queer little freckled face.

Now which is better, I couldn't say
If the Lord should ask me to choose today;
    If He should put in a call for me
    And say: "Now what shall your order be,
    A boy or girl? I have both in store—
    Which of the two are you waiting for?"
    I'd say with one of my broadest grins:
    "Send either one, if it can't be twins."

I've heard it said, to some people's shame,
They've cried with grief when a small boy came.
    For they wanted a girl. And some folks I know
    Who wanted a boy, just took on so
    When a girl was sent. But it seems to me
    That mothers and fathers should be happy
    To think, when the stork has come and gone,
    That the Lord should trust them with either one.

Boy or girl? There can be no choice;
There's something lovely in either voice.
    And all that I ask of the Lord to do
    Is to see that the mother comes safely through.
    And guard the baby and have it well,
    With a perfect form and a healthy yell,
    And a pair of eyes and a shock of hair.
    Then, boy or girl—and its dad won't care.[52]

Edgar A. Guest

68

27. Boy or Girl?

In their book, *Cheaper by the Dozen*, Frank Bunker Gilbreth and Ernestine Gilbreth Carey tell how their parents, efficiency experts for industry, planned when they married to have twelve children. Probably it took twelve to challenge their abilities! At any rate, they ordered six boys and six girls, and that is exactly what they got. Few of us would have the courage and faith to put in such an order and expect the desired results!

A research report in a newsmagazine tells us that parents someday may be able to determine the sex of their child, depending upon when the male sperm unites with the female egg cell. It seems that the sperms carry the Y chromosomes, which produce boy children, are twice as numerous and faster than the "female" sperm or X chromosomes, while the X chromosomes live longer than Y carriers. Thus scientists have figured out a possible method of "putting in an order" for a boy or girl by choosing the time of conception.

Most of us, however, would prefer to leave to our Creator the choice of sex in our offspring. If the day ever comes when we can decide whether we want a boy or a girl, what color the eyes and hair, and whether the child will have creative, mechanical, or agricultural interests—that will be the day!

We have all heard stories of parents who planned for a boy or a girl, then when they did not receive what they asked for, took out their disappointment on the child. Untold damage was done to the developing personality of the child. Other parents have been equally cruel, imposing their own frustrated ambitions on a child to become a doctor or a teacher or a mathematician.

When we learn that a member is going to be added to our family, the sex has already been determined, along with all the other inherent possibilities of our child. Our child will surprise us many times with new abilities and interests. Our part is to help develop the exciting possibilities of the child's personality. Let us thank God for the coming babe—boy or girl.

> This is what the Lord says—
> he who made you, who formed you in the womb,
> and who will help you. . . .
> I will pour out my Spirit on your offspring,
> and my blessing on your descendants.
>
> *Isaiah 44:2, 3b*

WHAT IS A GIRL?

Little girls are the nicest things that happen to people. They are born with a little bit of angel-shine about them and though it wears thin sometimes, there is always enough left to lasso your heart—even when they are sitting in the mud, or crying temperamental tears, or parading up the street in mother's best clothes.

A little girl can be sweeter (and badder) oftener than anyone else in the world. She can jitter around, and stomp, and make funny noises that frazzle your nerves; yet just when you open your mouth, she stands there demure with that special look in her eyes. A girl is Innocence playing in the mud, Beauty standing on its head, and Motherhood dragging a doll by the foot.

Girls are available in five colors—black, white, red, yellow, or brown, yet Mother Nature always manages to select your favorite color when you place your order. They disprove the law of supply and demand—there are millions of little girls, but each is as precious as rubies.

God borrows from many creatures to make a little girl. He uses the song of a bird, the squeal of a pig, the stubbornness of a mule, the antics of a monkey, the spryness of a grasshopper, the curiosity of a cat, the speed of a gazelle, the slyness of a fox, the softness of a kitten, and to top it all off He adds the mysterious mind of a woman.

A little girl likes new shoes, party dresses, small animals, first grade, noisemakers, the girl next door, dolls, make-believe, dancing lessons, ice cream, kitchens, coloring books, makeup, cans of water, going visiting, tea parties, and one boy. She doesn't care so much for visitors, boys in general, large dogs, hand-me-downs, straight chairs, vegetables, snowsuits, or staying in the front yard. She is loudest when you are thinking, the prettiest when she has provoked you, the busiest at bedtime, the quietest when you want to show her off, and the most flirtatious when she absolutely must not get the best of you again.

Who else can cause you more grief, joy, irritation, satisfaction, embarrassment, and genuine delight than this combination of Eve, Salome, and Florence Nightingale? She can muss up your home, your hair, and your dignity—spend your money, your time, and your temper—then just when your patience is ready to crack, her sunshine peeks through and you've lost again.

Yes, she is a nerve-racking nuisance, just a noisy bundle of mischief. But when your dreams tumble down and the world is a mess—when it seems you are pretty much of a fool after all—she can make you a king when she climbs on your knee and whispers, ''I love you best of all!''

Alan Beck[53]

28. It's a Girl!

Now, don't you think most people would rather have a boy than a girl?" a young woman wrote to a psychologist. "Wouldn't most parents rather hear the announcement, 'It's a boy'?"

This modern woman voices a question which sounds almost pagan to our ears. For heathen people often destroyed a girl-child, feeling that only a son brings real honor to a home. Girls in countries untouched by Christianity have often been despised, neglected, left to die, or bought and sold as property. In Bible times only the Hebrew nation, under God, gave woman a high status. The daughters of Job were spoken of as being fair; wise women gave advice to their nation in times of crises; mothers became dynamic forces in history as they protected and cared for such great leaders as Moses. A virtuous wife was considered of value "far above rubies."

Jesus depended upon good women to care for his needs, and he honored and respected women of his acquaintance. Women in the early church assumed leadership and made invaluable contributions to the Christian endeavor.

In answering the question about boys versus girls, the psychologist wisely pointed out that most fathers, although they enjoy the companionship of their sons, find a tender admiration in little daughters.

One father, Laurie Lee, in his late forties when his wife gave birth to their first child, wrote these words in an article, "Wonder of the Firstborn."

"Ever since I was handed this living heap of expectations, I can feel nothing but awe. She is, of course, just an ordinary miracle, but she is also the particular late wonder of my life. This girl, my child, this parcel of will and warmth, was born last autumn. . . . This moment of meeting seemed to be a birthtime for both of us, her first and my second life. Nothing, I knew, would be the same again, and I think I was reasonably shaken. Then they handed her to me, stiff and howling. I kissed her, and she went still and quiet, and I was instantly enslaved by her flattery of my powers. . . . I have got a daughter, whose life is already separate from mine. . . . She will give more than she gets, and may even later become *my* keeper."[54]

Although Jesus healed many persons, there are few accounts of his raising the dead to life. One of these stories, however, is of a little girl who was so ill that her father came to Jesus in great distress. By the time Jesus arrived at the home, the child had died. Luke, a physician himself, records that Jesus "took her by the hand and said, "My child, get up!" And she did, returning the warmth and joy to a household blessed with a daughter!

WHAT IS A BOY?

Between the innocence of babyhood and the dignity of manhood we find a delightful creature called a boy. Boys come in assorted sizes, weights, and colors, but all boys have the same creed: to enjoy every second of every minute of every hour of every day and to protest with noise (their only weapon) when their last minute is finished and the adult males pack them off to bed at night.

Boys are found everywhere—on top of, underneath, inside of, climbing on, swinging from, running around, or jumping to. Mothers love them, little girls hate them, older sisters and brothers tolerate them, adults ignore them, and Heaven protects them. A boy is Truth with dirt on its face, Beauty with a cut on its finger, Wisdom with bubble gum in its hair, and the Hope of the future with a frog in its pocket.

When you are busy, a boy is an inconsiderate, bothersome, intruding jangle of noise. When you want him to make a good impression, his brain turns to jelly or else he becomes a savage, sadistic, jungle creature bent on destroying the world and himself with it.

A boy is a composite—he has the appetite of a horse, the digestion of a sword swallower, the energy of a pocket-size atomic bomb, the curiosity of a cat, the lungs of a dictator, the imagination of a Paul Bunyan, the shyness of a violet, the audacity of a steel trap, the enthusiasm of a firecracker, and when he makes something he has five thumbs on each hand.

He likes ice cream, knives, saws, Christmas, comic books, the boy across the street, woods, water (in its natural habitat), large animals, Dad, trains, Saturday mornings, and fire engines. He is not much for Sunday school, company, schools, books without pictures, music lessons, neckties, barbers, girls, overcoats, adults, or bedtime.

Nobody else is so early to rise, or so late to supper. Nobody else gets so much fun out of trees, dogs, and breezes. Nobody else can cram into one pocket a rusty knife, a half-eaten apple, 3 feet of string, an empty Bull Durham sack, 2 gumdrops, 6 cents, a slingshot, a chunk of unknown substance, and a genuine supersonic code ring with a secret compartment.

A boy is a magical creature—you can lock him out of your workshop, but can't lock him out of your heart. You can get him out of your study, but you can't get him out of your mind. Might as well give up—he is your captor, your jailer, your boss, and your master—a freckled-face, pint-sized, cat-chasing bundle of noise. But when you come home at night with only the shattered pieces of your hopes and dreams he can mend them like new with two magic words—"Hi, Dad!"

Alan Beck[55]

72

29. *It's a Boy!*

Adam lay with his wife Eve, and she conceived and gave birth to Cain.
She said, "With the help of the Lord I have brought forth a man."

Genesis 4:1

Thus did the world's first mother celebrate the birth of a firstborn son—a man from
the Lord! A man, in the making, that is. Wordsworth has said, "The child is father to the
man." When we take into our arms our tiny boy-child, it is only natural to dream dreams—
a president, perhaps? Or a minister? Or a lawyer? Or a college professor?

But hold on there! Someone else has said that parents today are so eager to get
children into college, they sidestep the sandpile! We must remember the joys of raising a
boy are also ahead of us and the day of his boyhood are short and precious. One mother,
Miriam Sieber Lind, wrote these words while she was busy being the mother of boys:

Praise to the High One
  For giving me joys
Peculiarly sweet—
  I'm the mother of Boys!

Mud-puddles, torn blue-jeans;
  Toads, whistles, and worms;
The furred and the feathered
  And whatever squirms;
Black knuckles, bats, arrows,
  And thundering noise—
They're all in a day.
  For the mother of Boys.

But ah, 'tis a dear joy
  To turn the blue eyes
To the manifold wonders
  Of earth, sea, and skies.
And ah, 'tis a dear joy
  To watch small hand seize
The hand of his God
  In the knowledge of these....

Spare me, O High One,
  To praise Thee more—when
This mother of Boys
  Is a mother of Men![56]

°   °   °

I will exalt you, my God the King;
  I will praise your name for ever and
    ever.
Every day I will praise you
  and extol your name for ever and
    ever....
One generation will commend your
  works to another;
    they will tell of your might acts....

The Lord is gracious and
  compassionate,
  slow to anger and rich in love.
The Lord is good to all
  he has compassion on all he has
    made....
My mouth will speak in praise of the
  Lord.
Psalm 145:1, 2, 4, 8, 9, and 21a

73

WAITING WITHOUT WORRY

Because Thou hast promised to be with us always "even unto the end of the world," we know we are wrong when we think that as Thy human children we are forgotten. Yet it is hard to wait without worrying, and we begin to think that we are completely forsaken. Days are so long when we wait....

We need some sign from Thee that we are not alone in the waiting. Please stir our minds to remembrance of the beauty of spring after winter, the certain blossoming of the tree, the ripening of the fruit from the seed.

Let us know that each day we wait in trust is a part of the process of growing to maturity. Let worry leave our hearts as we learn the technique of waiting with our hands in Thine. Amen.[57]

Ruth C. Ikerman

"Wait for the Lord; be strong and take heart and wait for the Lord."

Psalm 27:14

30. *That Last Month*

I looked too early for the arrival of my first baby. Each day I thought, "This may be the day!" And it wasn't. Don put in his appearance a few days late. Yet, I couldn't hold it against him, that he was tardy, for I have been told that I arrived in this world one month behind schedule!

The trouble was that I, in my inexperience, requested our young helper to come ahead of time. With little housekeeping in our trailer-home, we filled the waiting hours with novels, taking walks, making Christmas candles, and visiting. One day Mildred wrote to a friend, "Today all I did was sew on a button."

For some reason it never occurred to us that we might profitably spend time studying about child care! When the baby did come, we bathed him with the help of one baby book and looked everything else up in the index of Dr. Spock.

The last month can be a trial for my mother-to-be. "I'm tired of my dresses," one lady-in-waiting complained. "I'm even tired of reading," another sighed. Patience—an elusive virtue at best—makes a polite bow and goes off the stage that last month. Almost we would exchange places with the family cat, who has to wait only about two months for the birth of her litter!

How can we maintain our patience that last month?

(1) Keep on reading about baby care, cramming, if you please, for the coming tests. But don't worry—even the experts tell us that "we are our own experts" and that mother intuition is not a lost art.

(2) Visit some new mothers and watch them give baths or fix formulas. Spend a little time now and then visiting your neighbors. Make a few calls on older friends and shut-ins, sharing the joy of your coming expectations. Don't choose someone, however, who will fill your mind and dismal stories.

(3) Get some really entertaining books from the library on some subject which interests you.

(4) Pursue your hobbies. If you enjoy cooking, make something fancy. If you have a freezer, stash away some goodies for your husband during your hospitalization. Do something with a flourish, if only prettying up the house!

(5) Take walks with your husband, or go for an occasional drive, or maybe go out for dinner if the budget will allow it.

Even then you will need to ask God for patience. Here is a prayer, written by a man many years ago, but helpful to women today:

"Take from us, O God, all tediousness of spirit, all impatience and unquietness. Let us possess ourselves in patience . . . through Jesus Christ our Lord. Amen."[58]

Jeremy Taylor, 1613-1667

FATHER, HEAR US

Father, hear us, we are praying,
Hear the words our hearts are saying,
We are praying for our children.

Keep them from the powers of evil,
From the secret, hidden peril,
Father, hear us for our children.

From the whirlpool that would suck them,
From the treacherous quicksand, pluck them,
Father, hear us for our children . . .

Through life's troubled waters steer them,
Through life's bitter battle cheer them,
Father, Father, be Thou near them.

Read the language of our longing,
Read the wordless pleadings thronging,
Holy Father, for our children.

And wherever they may bide,
Lead them home at eventide.[59]

Amy Carmichael

Acknowledgments

1. From *Such Thoughts of Thee*. Copyright 1952 by Herald Press, Scottdale, Pa.

2. From *Christian Parents Baby Book*, p. 4. Copyright 1955 by Herald Press, Scottdale, Pa.

3. From the book *A Chain of Prayer Across the Ages*, p. 137, compiled by Selina F. Fox. Published by E. P. Dutton & Co., Inc., and reprinted with permission.

4. From *The Book of Common Prayer*, p. 273.

5. "Ruined St. Stephen's Walbrook, London" from *Uncommon Prayers*, p. 117, by Cecil Hunt. American edition arranged by John Wallace Suter. Used by permission of The Seabury Press, New York, N.Y., and by permission of Hodder and Stoughton, Ltd., London, England.

6. *Your New Baby and You*. The Public Affairs Committee, Grosset and Dunlap, N.Y. 1966.

7. From *The Old Testament and the Fine Arts*, p. 280, by Cynthia Pearl Maus. Harper and Brothers, New York, N.Y. 1954.

8. Adapted from the book *A Chain of Prayer Across the Ages*, p. 263, compiled by Selina F. Fox. Published by E. P. Dutton & Co., Inc., and reprinted with permission.

9. William H. Genne. *Husbands and Pregnancy*. Association Press, New York, N.Y. 1956.

10. From *The Cross Is Lifted*, p. 33, by Chandran Devanesen. Friendship Press, New York, N.Y. 1954. Used by permission.

11. Used by permission of the author, Doris E. Schrock.

12. From the *Textbook of Obstetrics and Obstetric Nursing*, by Mae M. Bookmiller, R.N., and George Loveridge Bowen, M.D. W.B. Saunders Co., Philadelphia, Pa. 1954.

13. From *Chicago Poems* by Carl Sandburg. Copyright 1916 by Holt, Rinehart and Winston, Inc. Copyright 1944 by Carl Sandburg. Reprinted by permission of Holt, Rinehart and Winston, Inc., New York, N.Y.

14. Used by permission of Jeanne Nuechterlein.

15. From the *New Testament in Modern English*, © J. B. Phillips, 1958. Used by permission of The Macmillan Company.

16. *Bet It's a Boy* by Betty Bacon Blunt. Grosset and Dunlap, New York, N.Y. 1940.

17. From *The New English Bible*. © the Delegates of the Oxford University Press and the Syndics of the Cambridge University Press, 1961. Used by permission.

18. From *Uncommon Prayers*, p. 35, by Cecil Hunt. American edition arranged by John Wallace Suter. Used by permission of The Seabury Press, New York, N.Y., and by permission of Hodder and Stoughton, Ltd., London, England.

19. From *The New English Bible*. © the Delegates of the Oxford University Press and the Syndics of the Cambridge University Press, 1961. Used by permission.

20. From *Poems for Mothers* by Phyllis C. Michael. Zondervan Publishing House, Grand Rapids, Mich. 1963. Used by permission.

21. From *The World's Best Poetry, Vol. I: Of Home: Of Friendship*. John D. Morris and Company, Philadelphia, Pa. 1904.

22. Actual experience of Mrs. Paul Bowers, Iowa City, Iowa, who gave us permission to tell her story.

23. *Childbirth Without Fear* by Grantly Dick Read, M.D. © 1944. Harper and Brothers, New York, N.Y.

24. From the book *A Chain of Prayer Across the Ages* compiled by Selina F. Fox. Published by E. P. Dutton & Co., Inc., and reprinted with permission.

25. By Miriam Sieber Lind. Used by permission of the author.

26. These two prayers from *Uncommon Prayers*, pp. 99, 64, by Cecil Hunt. American edition arranged by John Wallace Suter. Used by permission of The Seabury Press, New York, N.Y., and by permission of Hodder and Stoughton, Ltd., London, England.

27. Reprinted by permission of *Ladies' Home Journal*. Copyright 1958 by Curtis Publishing Company, Philadelphia, Pa.

28. Adapted from *The Book of Common Worship*, p. 114. Used by permission of the Church of South India and the Oxford University Press, New York, N.Y. 1963.

29. From the *Log of the Good Ship Grace*.

30. From *The Old Testament and the Fine Arts*, p. 326, by Cynthia Pearl Maus. Harper and Brothers, New York, N.Y. Used by permission.

31. From "Parental Love Greatest Gift?" by Patricia McCormack. UPI.

32. As listed in a pamphlet from the National Association for Mental Health, Inc., New York, N.Y.

33. From *The Cross Is Lifted*, p. 36, by Chandran Devanesen. Friendship Press, New York, N.Y. Used by permission.

34. See "The Expectant Mother: Why Do I Feel So Tired?" by Keith P. Russell, M.D., in *Redbook*, June 1966.

35. See *Preparing for Childbirth* by Frederick W. Goodrich, Jr., MD. Prentice-Hall, Inc., Englewood Cliffs, N.J. 1966.

36. From *Prayers of the Spirit*, by John Wallace Suter. Copyright 1943 by Harper and Row, Publishers, Incorporated, New York, N.Y. Used by permission of the publishers.

37. Used by permission of Theo Oxenham, Worthing, England.

38. From *Living Letters*, The Paraphrased Epistles, Tyndale House Publishers, Wheaton, Ill. Used by permission.

39. From *Mr. Jones, Meet the Master*, p. 75, by Peter Marshall. Fleming H. Revell Company, Westwood, N.J. Used by permission.

40. From *Uncommon Prayers*, p. 143, by Cecil Hunt. American edition arranged by John Wallace Suter. Used by permission of The Seabury Press, New York, N.Y., and by permission of Hodder and Stoughton, Ltd., London, England.

41. From *Faith at Work* magazine.

42. From *Prayers of a Homemaker*, p. 63, by Ruth C. Ikerman, Copyright © 1966 by Abingdon Press, Nashville, Tenn. Used by permission.

43. From "In Memoriam," Stanza LIV, from the *Complete Poetical Works of Alfred Lord Tennyson*. Used by permission of the Houghton Mifflin Co., Boston, Mass.

44. From *Parents' Magazine's Baby Care Manual*, p. 15. Used by permission.

45. From *The Infant World* by Beth Day. Copyright by Beth Day. Reprinted by permission of Paul R. Reynolds, Inc., New York, N.Y.

46. From a Johnson & Johnson advertisement in *Parents' Magazine's Baby Care Manual*. Used by permission of Johnson & Johnson. New Brunswick, N.J.

47. From *The New English Bible*. © the Delegates of the Oxford University Press and the Syndics of the Cambridge University Press, 1961. Used by permission.

48. From *Mr. Jones, Meet the Master*, p. 175, by Peter Marshall. Fleming H. Revell Company, Westwood, N.J. Used by permission.

49. *Adventure to Motherhood*, by J. Allan Offen, M.D. Audio Visual Education Co. of America, Inc., Washington, D.C. 1964.

50. From *Homely Verses of a Home Lover*. Used by permission of Ward Lock & Co., Ltd., London, England.

51. *Mother and Child in Modern Art*, by Hooten and Kaiden. Meredith Publishing Co., Des Moines, Iowa.
52. From *Collected Verse of Edgar A. Guest*, Reilly & Lee (Henry Regenery Co.), Chicago, Ill. Used by permission.
53. Copyrighted by New England Mutual Life Insurance Company, 1950. Used by permission.
54. From *The Firstborn* by Laurie Lee. Copyright © 1964 by Laurie Lee. Used by permission.
55. Copyrighted by New England Mutual Life Insurance Company, 1950. Used by permission.
56. Used by permission of the author, Miriam Sieber Lind.
57. From *Prayers of a Homemaker*, p. 51, by Ruth C. Ikerman. Copyright © 1966 by Abingdon Press, Nashville, Tenn. Used by permission.
58. From *Uncommon Prayers*, p. 69, by Cecil Hunt, American edition arranged by John Wallace Suter. Used by permission of The Seabury Press, New York, N.Y., and by permission of Hodder and Stoughton, Ltd., London, England.
59. From *Gold Cord* by Amy Carmichael. Used by permission of the Christian Literature Crusade, Inc., Fort Washington, Pa.

All efforts have been made to find the owners and secure permissions for copyrighted material used in this book. In case of any oversight the publisher will be deeply grateful to be informed.

The Author

Born in Harrisonburg, Virginia, Helen Good Brenneman spent her childhood years near Hyattsville, Maryland, a suburb of Washington, D.C. She studied at Eastern Mennonite and Goshen colleges, and worked for four years as a clerk in the U.S. Department of Agriculture. Always interested in writing, Helen longed as a girl to become a newspaper reporter, but later found herself instead writing articles, stories, women's inspirational talks, and devotional books.

Following her marriage to Virgil Brenneman in 1947, the couple served a year in a refugee camp operated by the Mennonite Central Committee in Gronau, Germany, before going to Goshen, Indiana, where her husband studied for the ministry. They served for ten years in two pastorates, at Iowa City, Iowa, and Goshen, Indiana. Virgil was executive secretary of Mennonite Camping Association and regional representative of International Students, Inc. The Brennemans are the parents of two boys and two girls, as well as a foster daughter.

Other books by Mrs. Brenneman are *But Not Forsaken, Meditations for the New Mother,* the January section of *Breaking Bread Together* edited by Elaine Sommers Rich, *My Comforters, To the New Mother, The House by the Side of the Road, Ring a Dozen Doorbells, Marriage: Agony and Ecstasy, Learning to Cope,* and *Morning Joy.*